ISBN 978-1-334-30345-6
PIBN 10576892

This book is a reproduction of an important historical work. Forgotten Books uses state-of-the-art technology to digitally reconstruct the work, preserving the original format whilst repairing imperfections present in the aged copy. In rare cases, an imperfection in the original, such as a blemish or missing page, may be replicated in our edition. We do, however, repair the vast majority of imperfections successfully; any imperfections that remain are intentionally left to preserve the state of such historical works.

1 MONTH OF
FREE
READING

at

www.ForgottenBooks.com

By purchasing this book you are eligible for one month membership to ForgottenBooks.com, giving you unlimited access to our entire collection of over 700,000 titles via our web site and mobile apps.

To claim your free month visit:

www.forgottenbooks.com/free576892

English
Français
Deutsche
Italiano
Español
Português

www.forgottenbooks.com

Mythology Photography **Fiction**
Fishing Christianity **Art** Cooking
Essays Buddhism Freemasonry
Medicine **Biology** Music **Ancient
Egypt** Evolution Carpentry Physics
Dance Geology **Mathematics** Fitness
Shakespeare **Folklore** Yoga Marketing
Confidence Immortality Biographies
Poetry **Psychology** Witchcraft
Electronics Chemistry History **Law**
Accounting **Philosophy** Anthropology
Alchemy Drama Quantum Mechanics
Atheism Sexual Health **Ancient History**
Entrepreneurship Languages Sport
Paleontology Needlework Islam
Metaphysics Investment Archaeology
Parenting Statistics Criminology
Motivational

MODEL RELATIVISM:
A SITUATIONAL APPROACH TO MODEL BUILDING

Gary L. Lilien

November 1974   WP 755-74

MODEL RELATIVISM:
A SITUATIONAL APPROACH TO MODEL BUILDING

Gary L. Lilien

November 1974   WP 755-74

Acknowledgments

This paper grew out of many conversations -- contributors and influences are quite numerous. Special thanks are due to J. Morgan Jones, Donald G. Morrison, and Ambar G. Rao.

ABSTRACT

A model is not a theory. A theory implies "best possible" representation of a situation and should, (for a given analyst, at least), be
unique. An analyst, however, may build several "right" models of a particular situation, each for a different use or user. Model relativism,
the explicit consideration of the use and user in model development, has
important implications for building models, for implementing those models
and for developing teaching programs. Some of those implications are
explored in this paper.

1. Introduction

Why are so many models built and so few used? There are many answers
to this question, and I won't try a complete diagnosis here. However, I
hope to provide some insight into two aspects of that question:

(a) Why do some models seem doomed to failure from conception?

(b) What do we (I) mean by "used"?

Much has been written about modelling and model-building. Urban [6] cites
much of the related literature; the reference list of that paper is useful
for those studying the modelling process. My favorite treatment
of this theme is included in the chapters of Ackoff and Sasieni [1] which
treat problem recognition, modelling, testing, implementation and control.
The reader can keep his own most helpful model-writer in mind; they all
suffer from the same pedagogic weakness -- they help good modellers be
better modellers and don't do nearly as much for the "have-nots".

Why? I think the answer lies in the reason our model-writer chooses
to write on the subject in the first place. He has had years of experience
working on a large enough variety of problems to provide many of what he
classifies as "good" as well as "not so good" experiences. Then, as compul-
sive analysts will do, he has performed a discriminant analysis (formal or
informal) and has tried to determine the critical factors in his successful
works. In so doing he describes what, for him, is a successful pattern.
So far, okay. But in trying to transfer that knowledge, he is, I believe,
destined to fail.

I do not believe one can really learn from the experience of another,
and herein lies the problem. The brilliant, abstract principles that the
model-writer describes have the richness of his experiences behind them

when he rereads them. That is precisely because he has had those experiences. The naive reader, confronted with the same principles, finds them
bland truisms, and rather abstract as well. He has no such experience base
to put meat on these abstract principles.

A favorite principle of mine is that one should analyze any problem-
situation thoroughly before suggesting a solution strategy. That analysis,
if done carefully, will unearth some "special structure" which will greatly
facilitate solution. For example, consider allocating a fixed advertising
budget among areas with general response curves -- a very tough problem!
However, if those curves are found to be concave, the solution -- equating
marginal returns -- is just about trivial. My special structure principle,
read objectively, is as trite and seemingly devoid of operational content
as any I've encountered, yet it has tremendous importance for me. In successful work, I've consciously sought the "special structure" and have usually
located it.

The above can be viewed as a caveat. I will be describing my views of
modelling here. They seem profound and extremely insightful to me. They
may appear trite and obvious to the reader. By my argument above, I can,
at best, hope to reach a limited audience so I beg the reader's indulgence.

II. Model Relativism vs. Model Absolutism

I define the terms in this section's title as follows:

Model Absolutism (MA): that school of thought which would have
                        one believe that (only) one model best
                        describes a situation.

The followers of this school feel there is a one-to-one relationship
between a model and a theory. Since only one model (the best, in an

both the user (technically skeptical
manager versus sophisticated analyst,
e.g.) and the use (long range planning
versus short range scheduling, e.g.).

The MRist says, "Nonsense!" to the MAist model-theory association.
He believes, for example, that the best "theory" of consumer behavior
currently available, while useful to researchers, perhaps should not be
proposed for use in a particular situation where the marketing manager or
decision maker can't understand it and thus won't use it. The best representation of consumer behavior which the manager can understand, accept and
feel comfortable with can be the best model in an MR sense. We assume that
if we remove the main barriers-to-use (understanding and applications diffi-
culties) then the manager may use the model. Clearly, if after believing
in the model, the manager's model-budget runs out, he won't use it. The
barrier issue has been partially discussed by Little [3], through his "adap-
tive", "easy to understand" and "controllable" model criteria. What the
MRist would add is that the model design should adapt to changing users as
well as to changing situations.

Another issue under the general heading of barriers is that of "face
validity". A model that tracks and predicts well may not include one or
more variables a manager considers important. The excluded variable may

for instance be highly correlated with an included variable. No matter why -- the manager cannot accept the model because of this perceived omission. Then the model builder may be forced to include a variable which adds little or no power to the model to obtain managerial acceptance. Thus model complexity, as a constraint against use, can be either an upper or lower bound.

The MR viewpoint suggests why certain directions of modelling have been much less fruitful than others, both in a theory-development and in an implementation sense. Morrison [5] develops an insightful treatment of both these issues in the particular area of brand-switching models. He concludes that brand switching models of the types described in Massy, Montgomery and Morrison [4] cannot provide testable theories of brand choice behavior. At best, they are useful approximations to real behavior. And most, (except some recent developments in [2] and [6]), do not have explicit normative or decision-making implications. In addition, their mathematical structure makes them difficult for managers to understand and, hence, trust. They have therefore been little used for marketing decision making. Thus, these models rank low on theory-development and on implementation as well. Interest in this model area is waning.

Should we reject stochastic brand-switching models as useless? Perhaps not. They may, in fact, have several uses. First, considering some of the above mentioned normative work, they may have potential for management science-oriented marketing decision makers. If, in fact, the added richness (in terms of explicit modelling of individual differences and uncertainty) is sufficiently valuable to justify the additional management education needed for use, potential may exist here.

Another use exists as well. These models can provide valuable input for classroom discussion for teaching consumer behavior theory. Marketing students need to develop an understanding of the implications of buyer uncertainty on the purchase process. Studying stochastic models of buyer behavior can be very helpful in developing such an understanding, albeit in an abstract sense. The use of models for teaching programs will be developed more completely in the next section.

In this (somewhat digressive) discussion of brand switching models, we have described at least three uses. There may well be more, but those model uses are sufficiently different and of independent importance to list and review:

1. Pedagogic: for use in teaching and explanation. These models should be simple, unencumbered by details, easy to follow and only, perhaps, suggestive of real applications. Models should be designed to help structure thought at the expense of application-detail.

2. Managerial: the best model-representation of the situation still understandable and acceptable to the user. At one limit, it is equivalent to the Theory Representative use (below), at the other extreme it may be even simpler than the Pedagogic models above.

3. Theory Representative: the analyst's "best possible, state of knowledge, representation of the most vital aspects of the situation." This model is as complex as the situation demands; its complexity constrained only by the Principle of Parsimony.

Before leaving this topic, consider the historical development of the MAist tradition. Model building began with attempts to model fairly well behaved physical systems. The modelling problems that faced Galileo and Newton, complicated as they were, involved very few important variables in (analytically) simple relationships. There was little need for consideration of the user or use in model development.

Recently, more complicated man-machine systems with uncertain behavioral components have been modelled. Choices must be made about the variables to include, and exclude, the portions of the system to model and the level of detail to be considered. Different models of the same system are developed by different people. It sounds disturbing but is understandable: these "systems" are less well defined and different analysts attach different utilities to different system-aspects. Two analysts might easily come up with the same mathematical formulation of an assembly line balancing problem; the same formulation would be quite unlikely from two analysts working on an overall corporate strategy or planning problem.

Thus, we must consider analyst influence factors in explaining differences in models. Not only would the MRist hold that the best model of a situation depends on the proposed model-use, but, moreover, the "best" model could well depend, for complicated systems, on a qualitative analyst-style factor.

III. MODEL USE -- WHAT CAN IT MEAN?

The term "use" (referring to models) can mean different things. This ambiguity is at the heart of the communications problem faced by model builders and users. I list below a set of model uses, neither mutually exclusive nor exhaustive, but at least indicative of a range of uses:

1. Conceptualization: Often the first level of abstraction, a flow
   chart or simple, relationship-graph to indicate the nature of relationships. Models help in early steps toward alternate model development. Conceptual models are (generally) of more use to the model
   builder than the model user if user and builder are not the same
   person. One might place the bulk of classroom-models in the conceptual model class, as they are more helpful in thinking about reality
   than in decision making.

2. Description: Models can be used to describe how a system operates.
   Descriptive models contain no manager-controllable variables but
   are used to forecast events when independent variables are assumed
   known. A time series sales-forecast, Sales = f(Time), is a descriptive model, which may be used for budget or logistics planning.

3. Experimentation; Exploration: A model's response in alternative
   environments can be probed via experimentation. Experimentation is
   used to explore the response and characteristics of a system; models
   are developed to use in experiments when it is too costly, destructive,
   or otherwise infeasible to experiment on the real system. Exploration, as in heuristic programming is a systematic, sequential, way
   of trying out alternatives and improving actions. A model may be
   used as a vehicle on which to test a heuristic procedure.

4. Prescription: Models are developed to advise managers as to what they
   should do in a given situation -- thus they "prescribe." The output
   of an "experiment" or "exploration" may be a prescription or it
   may not. The model, Sales = f(Advertising), can be used for setting
   the levels of a controllable variable, advertising, when the related

fixed and variable costs are known. Prescriptive models contain controllable variables and can generally be manipulated to obtain "good" or "optimal" levels of those variables.

There are clearly other uses for models -- they can also be used to entertain and amuse (as dolls, model airplanes, e.g.). The important point here again is that different uses do exist.

For some, "use" of a model only implies replacement or elimination of human thought at some stage of a decision process. For the MRist "use" can mean aid in teaching or idea operation, aid, however minor, in decision making or aid in theory construction or testing.

IV. Implications for Teaching Programs

Management Scientists are generally called upon to train two distinct classes of students: future model developers and future model users. Since the two classes are almost disjoint, it is interesting that many schools of management do not treat them as such, either through course offerings or differing training programs. That observation aside, I state what I think we should do in the "best of all possible worlds" rather than what the ignorance of our committees on instruction or the stinginess of our alumni force us to do.

IV-1. The Role of Methods Courses in Management Training

Ask any future GM President in your own school of management what he hopes to get out of the quantitative methods course he is currently taking and he is likely to answer, "An 'A'." (The future GM Vice President would answer, "A 'B'.") Well, what should he answer? The reasons for his having

to take a "methods" course are frequently unclear to him, as well as to his
instructor who may think he is training graph theorists. He (they) may
think it relates to the school's goal of making a Renaissance Man of him.
I suggest there are some important reasons for these methods courses which
lead directly from the MR view of modelling.

Let us assume our beleaguered MBA candidate is studying queueing theory,
of all things, this week. He is presented with the M/M/1 queue in all its
analytic beauty. What use, M/M/1? I suggest there are at least three (and
we will assume here that our MBA goes on to study Transportation Networks
next and will see no more queues):

      A. Groundwork: The human mind best reasons from the simple
                to the complex and not vice versa, as we ask
                it to do eternally. It also reasons best from
                the specific to the general. If we give it
                the simplest, specific case to start with, it
                can go further most easily. If our MBA ever
                sees a waiting line problem again, he will know
                it is at least more complex than the one he has
                studied. He will also have some feel for the
                way one measures the performance of such things
                and will be in the right position to begin further
                analysis.

      B. Limits and Assumptions: As a manager, a little later on
                his path to the top, suppose one of his tech-
                nical analysts presents the results of his
                study, "Gas Station Site Sizing as an M/M/1

Queueing Problem." Our future oil baron asks
(after scouring his attic for his old notes):
"Don't customers arrive in cyclical patterns
during the day?" "Aren't service times for
big cars larger than those for little cars? or
motorcycles?" "What about customers who come
in for repairs?" "Don't customers usually get
a nasty glare after they ask for a clean wind-
shield when others are waiting (i.e., doesn't
expected service time go down with increasing
queue size)?" "Only one server?" And so forth.
The point is: he may not remember how or have the
tools to do the analysis himself, but he knows
what assumptions were made in the analysis he re-
viewed and he knows, therefore, the limitations
of that analysis. That analysis still may be
best, in an MR sense, but he always knows what
it can't do as well as what it can.

C. Discipline: I'm sure to get threatening mail for bringing
this one up. A great manager is analytic as well
as intuitive. He makes decisions after analyzing
and understanding a situation and its uncertainties
to the limits of his ability. He cannot tolerate
inconsistencies in his reasoning, or results that
"don't feel right" -- sloppy thinking of any kind.
Quantitative methods courses are a potential train-

ing ground for analytic, consistent, un-sloppy

thinking. Here one is forced to state assumptions,

show data, explore methods of analysis and report

results. A critic cannot just say, "I don't like

these results," because results follow from the

data, analysis and assumptions. The critic must

be more specific: suppose he doesn't like one

of the assumptions. Change it -- do the results

change? If not, no problem. If they do, argue

about the assumptions, only! The same holds for

data and methods. But the models and methods are

exposed and arguments of opinion are replaced by

arguments of substance. Quantitative methods

courses provide this in microcosm, and if taught

(and received) properly can be helpful in developing

analytic thinking.

IV-2. How Should Modelling be Taught to Builders

There are those who say either you have it or you don't. I am a gray area
man myself and I believe you can lighten the dark gray or make the dark gray
black if you work at it.

A. The MR concept must be made clear; that is, the use and user must
be included in the studies our Future Model Builder (FMB) performs. Give him
the Gas Station Queueing Problem, ask him (1) to model it so as to get the
concepts and dynamics of queues across to a class of MBA - general managers

in two lectures; (2) to model it for an experienced, but technically naive manager; (3) to model it for a Ph.D. dissertation on that particular queueing phenomonon.

He is likely to select the M/M/1 queue for (1), a simple simulation model (but one which satisfies the objection of our MBA in (III-12) for (2) and, hopefully do something very much more profound for (3). His response for (3) should probably include (2) as a special case just as (2) probably will include (1). But notice, three different models will still have been generated, even if they are hierarchical.

B. Most experienced modellers know a few examples of "excellent" models and know quite a few very "bad" models. Give a mixture of papers describing these models -- uncriticised. Let the FMB sort them himself. What criterion did he use for discrimination? Making this discrimination process explicit sharpens it and clarifies it and exposes it to criticism (and hence update and improvement).

C. Expose students to ill-structured situations in the form of cases, or, if possible, real organizational problems. Either by simulation (through cases) or in actual practice, different models, in the MR sense, should be developed for similar problems in different managerial or organizational settings.

D. Have the FMB take methods courses. He needs them for the same reason as the MBA-manager. But he also needs them to be secure in his analysis. Only if he has a complete set of keys can he feel certain that he should make a new one for his particular lock. And he might be tempted to use his sledge-hammer if it is the only "key" he has.

E. Have the FMB take readings courses. One understands models best
by forcing oneself to "work it out." Journals provide a playground for
analytic muscle-flexing. Readings courses can be used to develop both quantitative skills and appreciation and understanding of model building.

F. Builders generally have to "sell" their models at some time.
Have FMB's in a marketing models course (say) "sell" their services to
students involved in projects in a marketing management course. The results
could be interesting and valuable (if frustrating) for both sides.

Clearly this list is incomplete and much is debatable. But explicit
consideration of the MR approach should clarify and resolve many of the teaching issues that arise with respect to modelling.

V. The MR Recommendation: A Utility Theory for Models

Let's develop at least an implicit utility theory for models. A model's
use and acceptability have many dimensions and the weights (and interactions)
of those dimensions are relative to the situation, the use and the user.
Goodness of fit, predictive ability, parsimony are three such dimensions.
One could suggest others: robustness, ease of use in decision making, ease
of updating and maintenance, adaptiveness, costlines to support and operate,
etc. This list is far from complete and, of course, the factors could be
highly intercorrelated.

A model would be considered "dominant" if it ranked above all competing
models along all dimensions of evaluation. And a model would be "dominated"
if there existed at least one model which had a higher rating along all
dimensions. The dominated models could be eliminated from consideration
for a particular application while others could be considered.

This formalizes the informal procedure that model-critics have used
all along. It will allow arguments about particular models to reduce to
discussion of the relative importance of model attributes. And this is
the real issue.

It would be interesting to have "users" and "builders" rate a number
of well-known models and develop weights for the various dimensions. This
is work for the future, however.

Clearly, the explicit consideration of such a utility theory can only
be useful for "important" modelling efforts. However, at least an informal
consideration of these trade-offs could be valuable generally in improving
model building efforts.

VI. Conclusion

The MR or situational approach to model building, while perhaps not
offering much that is new, at least labels the alternatives. By naming
these alternatives, options can be more readily identified and modelling
objectives can be made more specific.

By providing labels, we can also make our arguments sharper and focus
only on points of disagreement. Modellers spend almost unlimited time arguing
that Model A is better than B without specifically labelling preference
criteria. Perhaps some hot air will be saved by this effort.

A real benefit may be in teaching programs. If teachers can better
clarify the different methods of building and using models, then perhaps
better modelers and higher implementation rates will result. I hope so.

REFERENCES

1. Ackoff, Russel L. and Maurice W. Sasieni. Fundamentals of Operations Research. John Wiley and Sons, New York, 1968.

2. Lilien, Gary L. "A Modified Linear Learning Model of Buyer Behavior," Management Science, Vol. 20, No. 7 (March 1974).

3. Little, J.D.C. "Models and Managers: The Concept of A Decision Calculus," Management Science, Vol. 16, No. 8 (April 1970).

4. Massy, William F., David B. Montgomery, and Donald G. Morrison. Stochastic Models of Buyer Behavior. MIT Press, Cambridge, MA 1970.

5. Morrison, Donald G. "The Use and Limitations of Brand Switching Models," presented at the Symposium on "Behavioral Science and Management Science in Marketing," Center for Continuing Education, University of Chicago, June 1969.

6. Nakanishi, Masao. "Advertising and Promotion Effects of Consumer Response to New Products." Journal of Marketing Research. Vol. 10 (August 1973).

7. Urban, Glen L. "Building Models for Decision Makers," Interfaces. Vol. 4, No. 3 (May 1974).

CPSIA information can be obtained
at www.ICGtesting.com
Printed in the USA
BVHW082246191118
533509BV00027B/2555/P